MW01101728

POND

WEBS OF LIFE

POND

Paul Fleisher

BENCHMARK BOOKS

MARSHALL CAVENDISH
NEW YORK

The author would like to acknowledge the work of Paul Sieswerda of the New York Aquarium for his careful reading of the manuscript; Jean Krulis for her elegant design work; and Kate Nunn and Kathy Bonomi for their capable editing. He would also like to express deep appreciation for the loving, patient support that his wife, Debra Sims Fleisher, has provided for many years.

Benchmark Books
Marshall Cavendish Corporation
99 White Plains Road
Tarrytown, New York 10591-9001

Illustration by Jean Cassels

Library of Congress Cataloging-in-Publication Data
Fleisher, Paul.
Pond / Paul Fleisher.
p.   cm.—(Webs of life)
Includes bibliographical references (p. 39) and index.
Summary: Examines the activities, plant and animal life, and climatic changes found in ponds.
ISBN 0-7614-0835-5 (lib. bdg.)
1. Pond ecology—Juvenile literature. [1. Pond ecology. 2. Ecology. 3.] I. Title. II. Series: Fleisher, Paul. Webs of life.
QH541.5.P63F58   1999   577.63—dc21 97-38071   CIP   AC

Photo Research by Ellen Barrett Dudley

Cover Photo: Photo Researchers, Inc./National Audubon Society/Alvin E. Staffan

The photographs in this book are used by permission and through the courtesy of: *Photo Researchers, Inc.*: Gregory K. Scott, 2, 20; Guy Gillette, 8-9; George & Judy Manna, 12(left); Robert Bornemann, 12(right); Rod Plank, 13; Peter G. Aitken, 14; Walter W. Timmerman, 15; Tom Branch, 18(top), 19; James Bell, 18(bottom); John Mitchell, 21; Stephon Dalton, 22, 23 (top); Michael Lustbader, 24; E. R. Degginger, 26-27; Steve & Dave Mazlowski, 27(right); Larry L. Miller, 28; J. H. Robinson, 29; Stephen J. Krasemann, 30(right), 32, 33(left); Stephen Collins, 34-35. *Photo Researchers, Inc./Science Source*: D. P. Wilson, 10(left); James Bell, 10(right); M. I. Walker, 11. *Animals Animals*: David J. Boyle, 6-7; S. Michael Bisceglie, 16-17; F. E. Unverhau FPSA, 23(bottom); Breck P. Kent, 25; E. R. Degginger, 26(left); Ken Cole, 30(left); Brian Milne, 31; Joe McDonald, 33(right).

Printed in Hong Kong

6   5   4   3   2   1

For my mother, Tresa Fleisher,
who taught me to care about the world
and the creatures living in it.

Let's walk down to the pond. A great blue heron stands silently in the shallows, waiting for a fish to swim by. The air is alive with the buzzing of insects and the singing of birds.

This small pond in rural New York is the center of a busy network of life. The plants growing here provide food for small animals like snails and minnows, and for larger ones like muskrats and geese.

Animals that eat plants are called primary consumers. Other animals—like the blue heron—are predators. They eat the animals that depend on the plants for food. Still other creatures are scavengers. They eat dead plants and animals and help recycle their bodies back into the pond.

Ponds may form when a stream is blocked by a landslide or a beaver dam or when a river changes course.

Many ponds in North America were formed at the end of the last ice age, about 11,500 years ago. When the glaciers melted away, they left hollows in the land. These hollows filled with water to become lakes and ponds.

Because pond plants need light, they only grow near the surface of the water or in the shallows. Algae are the simplest plants. Like all plants, algae use air, water, and the energy from sunlight to make food. This process is called photosynthesis (foe toe SIN thuh siss). Plants also make the oxygen that animals need to breathe.

Diatoms are beautiful single-celled algae. They reproduce by dividing. We can see them only if we look through a microscope. Millions of diatoms grow in the pond. They give it a greenish color.

This tiny, hollow ball is a colony of algae cells called volvox. It drifts through the water, gathering sunlight.

PILLBOX DIATOM

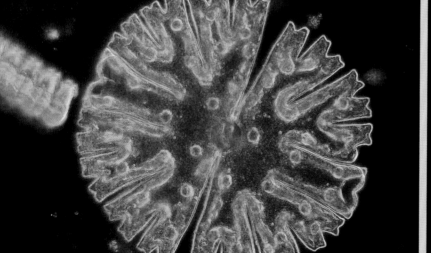

THE BIRTH OF A VOLVOX

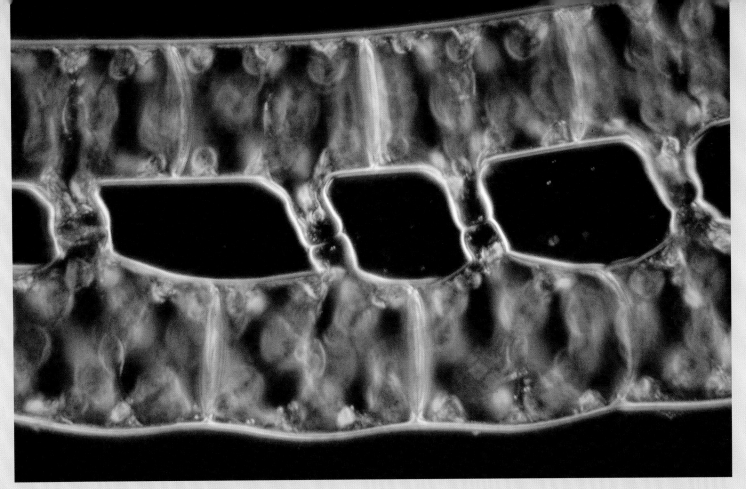

A CLOSER LOOK AT SPIROGYRA

Long threads of spirogyra, another algae, also grow in the pond. In summer, these algae form large mats that float on the water.

When algae use up most of the nutrients in the water, they begin to die. As the algae decay, they release nutrients back into the pond to be used again by other plants.

CATTAIL SHOOTS IN SPRING

ARROW ARUM

At the edges of the pond, cattail shoots poke up from last year's dry stems in early spring. By midsummer, the cattails will be four feet tall or more (1.2 meters).

Arrow arum leaves uncurl and spread themselves to catch the warm sunshine. The stems and leaves of the arrow arum are full of air bubbles that help them float.

Water lily pads drift on the surface at the end of long stems. Like arrow arum, their roots are anchored in the muddy bottom. Many small animals live on the underside of each broad lily pad.

WHITE WATER LILIES

THE POND IN SUMMER . . .

Pond life changes with the seasons. In spring, the sun warms the water. Algae and other plants grow rapidly, and animals become much more active.

Since warm water is lighter than cool water, it forms a layer above the colder, deeper water. If we wade into the pond, our feet feel cold, while our upper legs feel warm. The layers of warm and cool water stay in place all summer long!

Warm water holds much less

oxygen than cold water. On hot summer days, life in a pond can become very difficult. If the water gets too hot, fish may die from lack of oxygen.

In late fall, the air turns cold, and the water at the surface of the pond cools. The heavier cold water sinks to the bottom. This mixes the water and stirs up nutrients that were trapped at the bottom all summer. These chemicals will fertilize next year's plants.

15

When winter comes, many animals hibernate. Frogs, turtles, and salamanders bury themselves in the mud for a long sleep.

If the temperature drops below freezing, ice forms on the pond. Like a blanket, the ice keeps the water below at an even temperature. Fish spend the winter safely underneath.

When spring comes, the ice melts. Cold meltwater sinks to the bottom of the pond. This mixes the waters again. Nutrients are stirred up from the bottom once more, helping algae and other plants to grow.

17

COPEPODS WITH EGGS ON THEIR LEGS

DAPHNIA WITH EGGS INSIDE

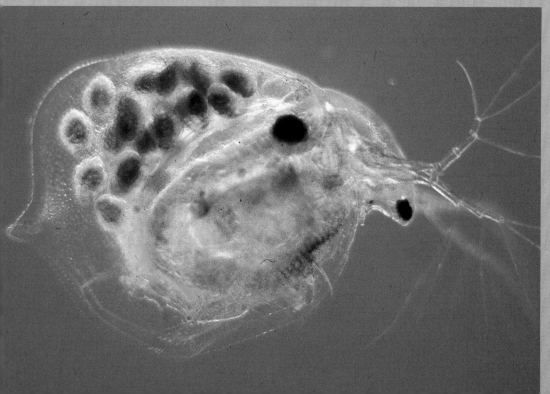

If we look very closely, we'll spy tiny creatures swimming among the algae. To see them clearly, we have to use a microscope.

Copepods are tiny shrimplike animals. They feed by filtering diatoms and other algae from the water. The female copepod carries her eggs in bundles on her hind legs.

Daphnia are sometimes called water fleas, but they are not insects. Like copepods, they are relatives of shrimp and crabs. Daphnia carry their babies in a pouch inside their shell.

Many small creatures live in the water—miniature jellyfish, insect larvae, and single-celled amoebas and paramecia. Together, these little swimming creatures are known as plankton.

Plankton is an important part of the pond's food chain. The plankton eats diatoms and bacteria in the water and is eaten by larger animals.

PLANKTON

A WHIRLIGIG BEETLE

The pond is also a home for many insects and insect larvae. A mosquito lays hundreds of eggs in the water. The eggs hatch into wiggling larvae. Most of the larvae are eaten by fish and other pond animals. Only a few will live to become adult mosquitoes.

Groups of whirligig beetles spin in circles on the surface of the water. Whirligig beetles have double sets of eyes. The upper half lets them see above the water, while the lower half lets them look below.

A giant water bug dives under-water to hunt for food. This bug is more than two inches (5 centimeters) long. It can even catch small fish and frogs. Be careful! The giant water bug can give your finger a painful bite.

GIANT WATER BUG SNAGGING A MEAL

DRAGONFLY

Dragonflies hover and dart above the water. They are powerful fliers. Dragonflies eat mosquitoes and other flying insects. They snare creatures such as mosquito larvae in their strong jaws.

The dragonfly's larvae live underwater. They, too, feast on mosquito larvae, gobbling thousands of them from the pond.

SWALLOW

During the day, swallows and other birds feast on flying insects. In the evening, bats swoop over the pond, catching more insects. Without these insect-eaters, there would be many more mosquitoes and biting flies to bother us when we visit the pond.

LITTLE BROWN BAT

Splash! A frog jumps into the water as we walk along the edge. Each spring the frogs call loudly to one another as they search for a mate.

BULLFROG

TADPOLE WITH LEGS

Frogs and toads lay clusters of jellylike eggs in the shallow water. The eggs hatch into tadpoles, which breathe with gills and swim in the water like fish. As the tadpoles grow, they change, or go through a metamorphosis (meh tuh MORE fuh siss). They grow legs and lungs and gradually lose their tails.

Most frogs and toads live on a diet of insects, along with worms and other small creatures. But an adult bullfrog is big enough to capture and eat small fish and young snakes and birds.

Littler fish dart about in the shallows, while larger ones lurk in deeper water. Bluegill sunfish hunt for worms, insects, and other small prey. In late spring, bluegills build round nests out of pebbles. After the female lays her eggs, the male bluegill guards them carefully until they hatch.

Bullhead catfish prowl the bottom. Their sensitive whiskers help them feel their way in the dark. Catfish eat live food such as worms and also scavenge for dead plants and animals that have sunk into the pond.

BLUEGILL SUNFISH

BROWN BULLHEAD

Largemouth bass are some of the biggest fish in the pond. They hide among the plants, waiting for unsuspecting prey. Bass eat fish, frogs, snakes, and even small mammals that have fallen into the water.

The slider turtle spends much of its time on a log, soaking up the warmth of the sun. Plants are its main source of food. If we get too close, the turtle slips back into the water where it is safe.

We often think of turtles as slow. But a snapping turtle is a quick and dangerous hunter. It can snap up fish and even young water birds with its powerful jaws.

RED-EARED SLIDER

BANDED WATER SNAKE

The water snake is not venomous—it doesn't have poison glands or fangs. But water snakes are agile hunters and excellent swimmers. You might see one gliding across the pond, with just its head above water. Water snakes eat frogs, fish, and other small pond animals.

MOTHER MALLARD AND DUCKLINGS

BELTED KINGFISHERS

Ducks and geese send ripples across the pond as they paddle with their webbed feet. They dip their heads below the surface to eat water plants and insects. Some ducks dive completely underwater in search of food.

A kingfisher sits high on a branch above the pond. When the kingfisher spots a fish, it folds its wings and dives into the water. It snatches the prey in its pointed beak.

A family of beavers harvests nearby trees, cutting them down with their sharp teeth. They drag the trees to the pond. The beavers eat the bark and use the logs and branches to build a large, dome-shaped lodge to live in.

BEAVERS

WHITE-TAILED DEER

Mammals from the surrounding woods and meadows visit the pond. If we stay very still and quiet, we might see deer come to the pond for a drink.

Perhaps we'll see a fox hunting birds or mice that live near the edge of the pond.

RACCOON

Raccoons visit the water's edge at night. This raccoon is on the lookout for frogs, crayfish, freshwater mussels, turtle eggs, or anything else good to eat.

RED FOX

Like plants and animals, ponds have life spans. A young pond usually has lots of open water. Year after year, plants and animals fall into the water when they die. As the dead matter decomposes, it becomes fertilizer for more plant growth. Heavy rains wash soil and nutrients from the surrounding land into the water. Little by little, the pond water fills in.

After many years, the pond will become a bog or a marsh. Finally, plants and soil fill in the pond completely. Grasses, shrubs, and trees grow where fish used to swim. The life cycle of the pond is complete.

Can you name the plants and animals in and around this pond?

Turn the page to check your answers.

Plants and Animals Found in and Around This Pond

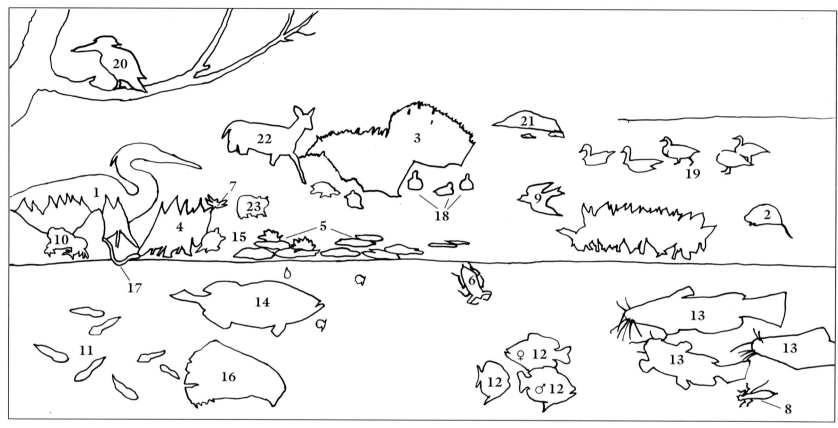

1. great blue heron	7. dragonfly	13. bullhead catfish	19. Canada goose
2. muskrat	8. dragonfly larva	14. largemouth bass	20. kingfisher
3. cattail	9. swallow	15. spotted turtle	21. beaver
4. arrow arum	10. bullfrog	16. snapping turtle	22. deer
5. water lily	11. tadpole	17. water snake	23. raccoon
6. giant water bug	12. bluegill sunfish	18. canvasback duck	

FIND OUT MORE

Fowler, Allan. *Life in a Pond*. Danbury, CT: Children's Press, 1996.

Kirkpatrick, Rena K. *Look at Pond Life*. Chatham, NJ: Raintree Steck-Vaughn, 1985.

Loewer, Peter H. *Pond Water Zoo: An Introduction to Microscopic Life*. New York: Atheneum Books for Young Readers, 1996.

Mason, Helen. *Life in a Pond*. Niagara Falls, NY: Durkin Hayes, 1992.

Schwartz, David M. *The Hidden Life of the Pond*. New York: Crown Books for Young Readers, 1988.

Tordjman, Nathalie. *The Living Pond*. Ossining, NY: Young Discovery Library, 1991.

INDEX

ABOUT THE AUTHOR

In addition to writing children's books, Paul Fleisher teaches gifted middle school students in Richmond, Virginia. He is often outdoors, gardening, walking, or just exploring. Fleisher has spent many happy hours fishing in the ponds of Maryland and Virginia.

The author is also active in organizations that work for peace and social justice, including the Richmond Peace Education Center and the Virginia Forum.